CROCHETING I BEGINNERS

A detailed beginner's guide with pictures to learn the amazing art of crocheting doilies patterns with beautiful projects for your home decor

Liz Rolland

Table of contents

CHAPTER ONE 4

    Introduction to Crocheting Doilies..............................4

    Why Crocheting Doilies is a Rewarding Craft...............7

CHAPTER TWO 11

    Essential Materials and Tools 11

    Understanding Basic Crochet Stitches 15

CHAPTER THREE 20

    How to read crochet patterns...................................20

    Choosing the Right Yarn and Hooks..........................24

CHAPTER FOUR 29

    Beginner-Friendly Doilies patterns 29

    Guide to making Simple Circle Doily 29

    Guide to making Simple Scalloped Edge Doily..........33

    Guide to making Petite Flower Doily 38

    Guide to making Lacy Granny Square Doily..............43

    Guide to making Heart-Shaped Doily........................49

CHAPTER FIVE 54

    Intermediate Doilies patterns...................................54

    Guide to making Irish Crochet Rose Doily.................54

    Guide to making Starburst Mandala Doily................61

    Guide to making Tapestry Crochet Doily 67

Guide to making Victorian Ruffled Doily 72

Guide to making Celtic Knot Doily 77

Guide to making Pineapple Lace Doily 82

CHAPTER SIX 87

Incorporating Beads and Embellishments into your doilies 87

Tips for Finishing and Blocking Doilies 91

Enhancing the Beauty of Your Finished Doilies 96

CHAPTER ONE

Introduction to Crocheting Doilies

Welcome to the magical realm of crocheted dolls! This book is a celebration of the time-honored craft of crocheting intricate and delicate doilies. These exquisite works of art have embellished residences, served as considerate gifts, and brought happiness to innumerable generations.

Crocheting dolls retains a special position in the affections of craft devotees all over the globe. With just a crochet tool and some yarn, you can transform simple strands into lace-like works of art. Whether you are a seasoned crocheter or a complete novice, this book will inspire and guide you through the process of creating breathtaking dolls that will be treasured for years to come.

In the following chapters, we will investigate the history and significance of crocheting doilies, dissect the basic techniques required to get started, and examine patterns spanning from beginner-friendly to advanced. Through precise, step-by-step instructions and accompanying images, you will gain the confidence to undertake a variety of projects, including refined centerpieces and holiday decorations.

You will discover the pleasure of combining colors, patterns, and motifs to create one-of-a-kind works that reflect your individual style and personality as you embark on this creative voyage. In addition, crocheting dolls can be a profoundly satisfying and therapeutic activity, enabling you to relax and find solace in the rhythmic motion of the hook.

Whether you choose to decorate your home with these delicate works of art, give them as gifts to loved ones, or even start a small business with them, the possibilities are only limited by your own creativity. Gather your supplies, embrace the meditative art of crochet, and allow your hands to bring these timeless patterns to life.

Prepare yourself for an unforgettable journey into the world of crocheted dolls. Let your imagination run wild, and may this book inspire you to create magnificent works that will endure for generations. Best crochet wishes!

Why Crocheting Doilies is a Rewarding Craft

Crocheting dolls is a satisfying hobby for a number of reasons.

1. Through their choice of colors, techniques, and patterns, crocheters are able to express their creativity when making dolls. Each puppet becomes a unique work of art that reflects the individual style and vision of its creator.

2. The completion of a crocheted doily can provide a profound sense of accomplishment. Seeing a basic skein of yarn transform into a delicate and intricate work of art is immensely satisfying.

3. Crocheting can be a meditative and therapeutic activity. The repetitive

motions of the crochet needle and yarn can alleviate tension and anxiety and promote relaxation.

4. Doilies are both useful and beautiful creations. They can be utilized as table centerpieces, table decorations, or as wall art. They are an excellent option for home decor or considerate presents for loved ones due to their versatility.

5. Crocheting stuffed animals is a portable hobby that can be enjoyed almost anywhere. Whether traveling, waiting for an appointment, or unwinding at home, you can transport your project with you and remain productive.

6. Crocheting dolls are accessible to crocheters of all skill levels, from novices to seasoned professionals.

There are easy patterns for those who are new to crochet, as well as difficult patterns for those who wish to improve their abilities.

7. Crochet dolls have a long history, connecting craftspeople to generations of artisans who have handed down their skills and techniques. By perpetuating this art form, artisans contribute to a long-standing tradition.

8. Crocheting dolls requires few materials, making it an inexpensive recreation. Yarn and crochet implements are comparatively economical, and a single ball of yarn can be used to create multiple dolls.

9. Community and Sharing: The crochet community is expansive and generous. By participating in local

meetings or online forums with other artisans, it is possible to share ideas, obtain inspiration, and foster a sense of camaraderie.

10. Crocheted dolls have the potential to become cherished heirlooms that are handed down through the generations. Handcrafted objects have sentimental value and provide a tangible link to our past.

In conclusion, crocheting dolls provides a satisfying and enriching experience. It allows for the expression of creativity, the creation of gorgeous and meaningful objects, and the formation of connections with others who share a passion for this timeless craft.

CHAPTER TWO

Essential Materials and Tools

A few essential materials and instruments are required to begin crocheting doilies. Here is a list of items you will need:

1. Crochet Hooks: Choose a set of crochet hooks in various sizes, as

different crochet hook sizes may be required for various undertakings. Depending on the yarn weight and desired doily size, the most frequently used hook sizes for dolls range from 1.5 mm to 2.5 mm.

2. Choose high-quality crochet thread or delicate yarn in a variety of colors for the yarn. Typically, crochet thread is used to create delicate and intricate dolls, whereas fine yarn can be used to create slightly larger, intricate items. To accomplish the desired effect, experiment with various yarn varieties and textures.

3. A pair of precise scissors is required for cutting yarn and weaving in ends after finishing a project.

4. This tapestry needle with a large eye is used to weave in stray yarn ends and unite crocheted segments.

5. Markers for Stitches Markers for stitches are useful for keeping track of threads and designating specific locations in your work, particularly when working with intricate patterns.

6. A flexible measuring tape allows you to precisely measure the dimensions and gauge of your work.

7. Blocking is an essential procedure for shaping and flattening your finished doilies. You can moisten your work with blocking mats, T-pins, and a spray container before shaping and allowing it to dry.

8. Invest in a collection of crochet pattern books or search online for

patterns. Print or save the patterns you intend to work on on a digital device for simple reference.

9. Notebook and Pen: Keep a crochet journal to record your ideas, notes, and pattern modifications. This allows you to monitor your progress and create a resource for future endeavors.

10. Crocheting dolls can be a time-consuming process, so ensure you have a comfortable chair and adequate illumination to prevent muscle strain and eye fatigue.

11. Some crocheters find additional accessories useful, such as a yarn receptacle to prevent yarn from tangling, a project pouch to transport your work on the go, and ergonomic handles for crochet tools to reduce

hand fatigue during extended crocheting sessions.

Possessing these essential materials and equipment will send you on the path to creating exquisite dolls. As you acquire experience, you may discover additional tools or methods that suit your personal preferences and manner. Best crochet wishes!

Understanding Basic Crochet Stitches

To create stunning crocheted dolls, one must have a foundational understanding of fundamental crochet stitches. Mastering the characteristics of each seam will enable you to create a variety of textures and patterns in your creations. Here is an outline of the basic crochet stitches:

1. The chain pattern is the beginning point for the majority of crochet endeavors. It produces a series of interconnected coils and serves as the base for subsequent sutures. Additionally, chains can be used to create spaces and serve as a pivot point in your work.

2. Single Crochet (sc): The single crochet pattern is basic and widely used. It yields a dense and compact fabric. Insert the hook into the desired stitch, yarn over, pull through one loop, then crochet over again and pull through both loops on the hook.

3. The Half Double Crochet (hdc) is taller than the single crochet but shorter than the double crochet. It produces a fabric that is slightly looser

and is created more quickly than single crochet. To create a half double crochet, yarn over, insert hook into desired stitch, yarn over again, pull through loop, yarn over, and pull through all three loops on hook.

4. Double crochet (dc) is a taller design that produces an airy, transparent fabric. To create a double crochet, yarn over, insert the hook into the desired stitch, yarn over again, pull through a loop, yarn over and pull through the first two loops on the hook, and then yarn over and pull through the last two loops on the hook.

5. Treble Crochet (tr): Even taller than double crochet, treble crochet creates a very transparent and intricate fabric. To create a treble crochet, yarn over

twice, insert the hook into the desired stitch, yarn over once more, pull through a loop, yarn over and pull through the first two loops on the hook, yarn over and pull through the next two loops, and then yarn over and pull through the last two loops.

6. Slip Stitch (sl st): The slip stitch is utilized to join rounds, create clean edges, and finish a project. Insert the hook into the desired stitch, yarn over, and draw the yarn through the stitch as well as the loop on the hook.

Understanding these fundamental crochet techniques will allow you to read crochet patterns and experiment with various combinations to create gorgeous textures and designs for your dolls. You will gain confidence and be prepared to tackle more intricate and advanced crochet techniques as you gain experience. Best crochet wishes!

CHAPTER THREE

How to read crochet patterns

With practice and a comprehension of the symbols and abbreviations, you will be able to read and follow crochet patterns with simplicity. The following is a detailed guide on how to interpret crochet patterns.

1. Start with the Materials List. The pattern will typically begin with a list of materials, including the recommended yarn, hook size, and any additional tools and embellishments.

2. Crochet patterns use standard abbreviations to symbolize the various stitches. ch (chain), sc (single crochet), hdc (half double crochet), dc (double crochet), tr (treble crochet), and sl st (slip stitch) are common crochet

abbreviations. Before you begin, familiarize yourself with these abbreviations.

3. Read the Stitch Key. The majority of patterns include a stitch key that describes the symbols used in the pattern chart. If the pattern includes a chart or diagram, consult the stitch key to identify each symbol.

4. Check the Gauge: Gauge is the number of stitches and rows per inch when using the recommended tool and yarn. It guarantees that the completed product will match the dimensions specified in the pattern. Take the time to crochet a gauge swatch prior to beginning the actual endeavor.

5. Follow the Written Instructions Each row or round of the pattern will include

written instructions. These directions outline which knots to create and in what order. For instance, "Chain 3, dc in the next stitch, ch 2, sk 2 sts, dc in the next stitch" instructs you to chain 3, double crochet in the next stitch, chain 2, skip the next two stitches, and then double crochet in the next stitch.

6. Refer to Diagrams and Charts (if available): Some patterns may include diagrams or charts that depict the pattern threads. Use the chart in addition to the written instructions if you prefer visual instructions.

7. Observe Repeat Sections Crochet patterns frequently contain repeat sections, denoted by asterisks (*) or square brackets. For instance, "Repeat [dc in the next 3 sts, ch 1] five times"

instructs you to repeat the sequence "dc in the next three stitches, ch 1" five times.

8. Some patterns may include special instructions for particular sections or techniques. Before proceeding, read these attentively.

9. completing Instructions: The pattern will conclude with instructions for completing the project, including how to fasten off, weave in ends, and block (if necessary).

10. If the pattern involves intricate thread sequences or contouring, use stitch markers to keep track of specific stitches or sections.

Remember that practice makes deciphering crochet patterns more intuitive. As you gain confidence in your crochet skills, you should progress from uncomplicated patterns to increasingly complex endeavors. Best crochet wishes!

Choosing the Right Yarn and Hooks

Selecting the proper yarn and crochet implements is essential for the success of your crochet endeavors. The appearance, texture, and size of your crocheted dolls are determined by the combination of yarn weight and hook size. Here are some guidelines to assist you in making wise decisions:

1. Thread Weight:

• Yarn is available in a range of weights, from extremely delicate (lace weight) to extremely thick. Each weight has its own characteristics and can be used for a variety of endeavors.

• Fine yarn or crochet thread (lace weight or fingering weight) should be used for delicate and intricate dolls. A thinner textile produces intricate details and a lacy look.

• Choose sport weight or light worsted weight yarn for slightly larger and more substantial dolls.

• Avoid using weighty or dense yarn for dolls, unless you want a robust and less delicate result.

2. Fiber Content:

• Consider the yarn's fiber content. Natural fibers such as cotton and bamboo can produce dolls that are gentler and more flexible, whereas synthetic fibers such as acrylic or nylon can provide durability and simple maintenance.

3. Hook Size:

• The size of the crochet tool determines the size of the stitches and the drape of the finished product.

• For intricate and delicate dolls made with fine yarn or crochet thread, use smaller steel crochet needles in the range of 1.5 mm to 2.5 mm.

• Use ordinary aluminum or plastic crochet tools measuring between 3.5 mm and 4.5 mm for sport weight or light worsted weight yarn.

• Always examine the yarn label for the recommended hook size. It serves as a decent starting point, but you may need to modify the attachment size based on the tension and desired size of the carriage.

4. Tension and Thickness:

• Pay careful attention to tension when crocheting. Tension refers to how securely or loosely you crochet, which can affect the size of your threads and the size of the finished figurine.

• Using the recommended hook and yarn, crochet a small swatch to determine your gauge. Determine whether the number of stitches and rows in a particular dimension (typically 4 inches/10 centimeters) corresponds to the pattern's gauge. If necessary, adjust your hook size to attain the precise gauge.

5. Color Options:

• Select colors that complement the design and function of your carriage. Classic and delicate are pastel colors, while bold and flamboyant colors can lend a modern touch.

6. Experiment and Enjoy Yourself:

• Don't be afraid to experiment with various fabrics, hooks, and color combinations to determine what works best for your preferred doll design.

Remember that the proper combination of yarn and hook will enhance the attractiveness and overall allure of your crocheted dolls. Explore various alternatives and locate the optimal solution for your projects. Best crochet wishes!

CHAPTER FOUR

Beginner-Friendly Doilies patterns

Here are some patterns for crochet dolls that are suitable for beginners:

Guide to making Simple Circle Doily

Material Required:

- Fine yarn or crochet thread • Crochet needle of 2.5 millimeters • Scissors

- Thread Needle

First, create a chain stitch (ch). Begin by tying a slip knot, then create a chain of six threads.

Second Step: Joining the Ring Insert your hook into the chain stitch closest to the slip knot and slip stitch to form a ring.

Step 3: Round 1 - Begin the Circle with a 3-chain foundation (this counts as your first double crochet) and 11 double crochets (dc) into the ring. You should have a total of 12 threads, including the initial chain-3.

Step 4: Round 2 - Increasing Stitches Chain 3 (this will be your first double crochet), then double crochet into the same stitch. Now, perform two double crochet stitches in each of the next eleven stitches around the ring. To complete the round, slip stitch into the top of the commencing chain-3. You should have a total of 24 sutures.

Step 5: Round 3 - Continuing the Increase Chain 3, double crochet in the same stitch. Perform 1 double crochet in the next stitch, then 2 double crochets in the following stitch. Repeat this pattern around the ring (1 dc, 1 dc, 2 dc). To complete the round, slip stitch into the top of the commencing chain-3. You should have a total of 36 sutures.

Step 6: Round 4: Final Increase Chain 3 (this will be your first double crochet), then double crochet in the same stitch. Perform 1 double crochet in each of the next 2 stitches, then 2 double crochets in the following stitch. Repeat this pattern around the ring (1 dc, 1 dc, 1 dc, 2 dc). To complete the round, slip stitch into the top of the commencing chain-3. You should have a total of 48 sutures.

Step 7: Round 5: Creating the Edging Chain 1 (does not count as a stitch), then single crochet 1 stitch in each stitch around the circle. To complete the round, slip stitch into the first single crochet thread.

Step 8: Fasten Off Leave the yarn with a tail after cutting. Pull the tail through the final coil on the hook and tighten. Employ a tapestry needle to weave in any stray ends.

Blocking is the ninth (optional) step. To shape and flatten your doily, you can gently saturate it and attach it to a blocking mat, stretching and molding it into a circle. Permit it to cure thoroughly prior to removing the pegs.

And that concludes it! Your straightforward circle doily is complete. You can create distinctive variations of this classic doily pattern by experimenting with various yarns and colors. Best crochet wishes!

Guide to making Simple Scalloped Edge Doily

Here is a step-by-step guide on how to make a straightforward doily with scalloped edges:

Material Required:

- Fine yarn or crochet thread • Crochet needle measuring 2.5 mm

- Scissors

- Thread Needle

First, create a chain stitch (ch). Begin by tying a slip knot, then create a chain of six threads.

Second Step: Joining the Ring Insert your hook into the chain stitch closest to the slip knot and slip stitch to form a ring.

Step 3: Round 1 - Begin the Circle with a 3-chain foundation (this counts as your first double crochet) and 11 double crochets (dc) into the ring. You should have a total of 12 threads, including the initial chain-3.

Step 4: Round 2 - Stitch Increases Chain 3 (this will function as your first double crochet), then double crochet into the same stitch again. Now, perform two double crochet stitches in each of the next eleven stitches around the ring. To complete the round, slip stitch into the top of the commencing chain-3. You should have a total of 24 sutures.

Round 3 of the scalloped edge In the same stitch, chain 1 (this does not count as a stitch) and single crochet 1 stitch. Skipping the next stitch, make five double crochets (5 dc) in the following stitch to create the first scallop.

Repeat the pattern below to produce a scalloped edge: To form the next scallop, skip 1 stitch, single crochet in the next stitch, skip 1 stitch, and then make 5 double crochets (5 dc) in the next stitch.

Continue this pattern around the circle to create a total of 12 scallops. To complete the round, slip stitch into the first single crochet thread.

Step 6: Fasten Off Leave the yarn with a tail after cutting. Pull the tail through the final coil on the hook and tighten. Employ a tapestry needle to weave in any stray ends.

Optional seventh step: blocking. To shape and flatten your doily, you can gently saturate it and attach it to a blocking mat, stretching and molding it into a circle. Permit it to cure thoroughly prior to removing the pegs.

In conclusion, there you have it! Your straightforward doily with scalloped edges is complete. The scalloped edge lends an elegant flourish to this traditional doily design. Feel free to experiment with various colors and textile types to create one-of-a-kind variants of this pattern. Best crochet wishes!

Guide to making Petite Flower Doily

Here is a detailed guide on how to make a Petite Flower Doily:

Material Required:

- Fine yarn or thread for crocheting
- 2.0 mm crochet needle
- Scissors

- Thread Needle

First, create a chain stitch (ch). Begin by tying a slip knot, then create a chain of six threads.

Second Step: Joining the Ring Insert your hook into the chain stitch closest to the slip knot and slip stitch to form a ring.

Step 3: Round 1 - Begin the Circle with a 3-chain foundation (this counts as your first double crochet) and 11 double crochets (dc) into the ring. You should have a total of 12 threads, including the initial chain-3.

Step 4: Round 2 - First Petal Chain 5 (this will be your first petal), then slip stitch into the same stitch where you made your final double crochet in

Round 1 (the first stitch of the round). This concludes the initial petal.

Fifth Phase: Creating the Petals To construct the remaining petals, repeat the following pattern: To create a petal, chain 5, then slip stitch into the next stitch of Round 1 (the next double crochet stitch).

Continue this pattern around the circle to produce a total of 12 petals. To complete the round, slip stitch into the top of the first chain of the chain-5 beginning chain.

Step 6: Round 3: Edging Chain 1 (does not count as a stitch); single crochet in the same stitch where you slip-stitched to join the previous round (the top of the first chain-5 of a petal).

Repeat the pattern below to construct the border: Make 7 double crochets in the next chain-5 space (the space between the petals), then 1 single crochet in the chain-5 space at the top of the next petal.

Continue this pattern around the circumference of the circle to create the scalloped edge between the petals. To complete the round, slip stitch into the first single crochet thread.

Step 7: Fasten Off Leave the yarn with a tail after cutting. Pull the tail through the final coil on the hook and tighten. Employ a tapestry needle to weave in any stray ends.

Optional eighth step: blocking To shape and flatten your doily, you can gently saturate it and attach it to a blocking mat, stretching and molding it into a circle. Permit it to cure thoroughly prior to removing the pegs.

In conclusion, there you have it! With its charming flower petal design, your Petite Flower Doily is complete. The doily can be utilized as a lovely receptacle, decorative element, or component of a larger crochet project. Experiment with various colors to produce one-of-a-kind variations of this endearing pattern. Best crochet wishes!

Guide to making Lacy Granny Square Doily

Here is a detailed guide on how to make a Lacy Granny Square Doily:

Material Required:

- Fine yarn or crochet thread • Crochet needle measuring 2.5 mm

- Scissors

- Thread Needle

Step 1: Begin a Granny Square
Construct a ring with a slip stitch and six chains.

Phase 2: Round 1 Chain 3 (this counts as your first double crochet), then work 2 double crochets (dc) into the ring (this counts as your first double crochet). This creates the initial aggregation of three dc. To create a corner space, chain two. Then, work three double crochet stitches into the ring, followed by another chain 2 to create the second corner space. This pattern should be repeated twice more to complete the round. You should have four clusters of three dc, with a chain-2 corner space between each cluster.

Step 3: Round 2 Slip stitch into the next two dc and the first corner space created by two chains. Chain 3 (this counts as your first double crochet), then make 2 double crochet stitches in the same corner space to create the first corner cluster. For the corner space, chain two. Create 3 dc in the same corner space, followed by 1 chain.

Repeat the pattern for the remaining three corners: In each of the remaining three corner spaces, work 3 dc, 2 chains, and 3 dc. Chain 1 and slip stitch into the top of the initial chain-3 to finish the round.

Step 4: Round 3 Slip stitch into the next two dc and the first corner space created by two chains. Make 2 double crochet stitches in the same corner space to form the first corner cluster, then chain 2 for the corner space. Create 3 dc in the same corner space, followed by 1 chain.

In the space between chain-1 clusters: Make 3 dc and 1 chain.

Repeat the pattern for the remaining three corners and sides: In each of the remaining three corner spaces, work 3 dc, 2 chains, and 3 dc. After completing each corner, chain 1 and work 3 dc in the next chain-1 space along the side. Continue with the pattern around, and join with a slip stitch to the top of the initial chain-3 to complete the round.

Step 5: Beyond Round Four Continue the pattern for Round 3, increasing the number of chain-1 spaces by one for each succeeding round. This will add additional intricate lace details to your crocheted square doily.

Optional sixth stage: edging To complete the doily, an edging can be added. You may use a simple scalloped edge, picots, or any other embellishment of your choosing.

Step 7: Fasten Off Leave the yarn with a tail after cutting. Pull the tail through the final coil on the hook and tighten. Employ a tapestry needle to weave in any stray ends.

Optional eighth step: blocking To shape and flatten your doily, you can gently saturate it and attach it to a blocking mat, stretching and molding it into a square. Permit it to cure thoroughly prior to removing the pegs.

And that concludes it! Your Lacy Granny Square Doily is complete, featuring a lovely lace pattern within a traditional granny square pattern. You can make several of these squares and sew them together to create a tablecloth or a decorative drape. Experiment with various colors to produce one-of-a-kind variations of this timeless pattern. Best crochet wishes!

Guide to making Heart-Shaped Doily

Here is a detailed guide on how to make a Heart-Shaped Doily:

Material Required:

- Fine yarn or crochet thread
- Crochet needle of 2.5 millimeters
- Scissors
- Thread Needle

Step 1: Beginning the Heart Form Chain 4 to start.

Second Stage: First Half of the Heart In the fourth chain from the needle, work three double crochets (dc). This forms the initial portion of the heart shape.

Step 3: Heart Center Chain 3 (this counts as the first double crochet of the second half of the heart), then work 3 additional double crochets in the fourth chain from the hook. This creates the heart's central depression.

Fourth Step: Second Half of the Heart Chain 1 (to form the heart's point) and then slip stitch 1 in the same chain space. This creates the heart's apex.

Step 5: Continuing with the Second Half Chain 1, then work three double crochet stitches in the same chain space. This constitutes the second portion of the heart.

Step 6: Round 1 - Outer Round Create the first corner cluster by chaining 3 and working 2 double crochets in the same chain space. For the corner space, chain 1. In the space created by one chain between the heart halves, work three double crochets and one chain.

Repeat the pattern for the remaining two corners: Make 1 double crochet, chain 1, followed by 3 double crochets, chain 1, in the next chain-1 space.

After the final corner, complete the round with three double crochets and one chain in the first corner space. To join the round, slip stitch into the top of the commencing chain-3.

Step 7: Round 2 - Outer Edging In the same corner space, chain 3 (this counts as the first double crochet) and make 1 double crochet. In the following chain-1 space, perform two double crochets.

Repeat the pattern below for the sides: Make 2 double crochets, 2 chains, and 2 double crochets in the next corner space. In the following chain-1 space, perform two double crochets.

Repeat the pattern below for the remaining two corners and the final side: Make 2 double crochets, 2 chains, and 2 double crochets in the next corner space.

To complete the round, slip stitch into the top of the commencing chain-3.

Step 8: Fasten Off Leave the yarn with a tail after cutting. Pull the tail through the final coil on the hook and tighten. Employ a tapestry needle to weave in any stray ends.

Blocking is the ninth (optional) step. To shape and flatten your doily, you can gently saturate it and attach it to a blocking mat, stretching and molding it into a heart. Permit it to cure thoroughly prior to removing the pegs.

And that concludes it! Your Heart-Shaped Doily is complete, featuring an endearing heart motif that is ideal for decorative purposes or as a considerate gift for a special someone. Experiment with various colors to generate distinct variations of this beautiful pattern. Best crochet wishes!

CHAPTER FIVE

Intermediate Doilies patterns

Here are some doll patterns for intermediate crocheters that will challenge and improve your skills:

Guide to making Irish Crochet Rose Doily

The creation of an Irish Crochet Rose Doily necessitates some knowledge of Irish crochet techniques. Here is a step-by-step guide on how to make a lovely Irish Crochet Rose Doily:

Material Required:

• Fine yarn or crochet thread in multiple colors (rose color, green for the foliage, and white for the doily background) • A crochet hook with a 2.5 mm gauge and a hook size of your choice

• Scissors

• Thread Needle

First, create the Rose Motifs. Typically, Irish crochet roses are created separately and then stitched onto the foundation of the doily. Using Irish crochet techniques, create a number of tiny and large rose motifs. You can find particular rose patterns and tutorials for Irish crochet in Irish crochet books and online resources.

Step 2: Preparing the Background for the Doily Begin with the white yarn (or a color of your choosing for the background of the doily) and construct a tiny circle using the magic ring or chain 4 and slip stitch to form a ring.

Step 3: Round 1 Chain 3 (this counts as your first double crochet), then double crochet 11 stitches into the ring. You should have a total of 12 threads, including the initial chain-3.

Step 4: Round 2 Chain 5 (this qualifies as the first double crochet and corner space created with two chains). Make 1 double crochet in the same stitch as the initial chain of five stitches. In the following pattern, perform two double crochets. In the following stitch, perform 1 double crochet.

This pattern is repeated for the remaining stitches in the round: Make 2 double crochet stitches in the next stitch, then 1 double crochet stitch in the next stitch.

In the following stitch, work 1 double crochet, 2 chains, and 1 double crochet to form the next corner. Repeat from * to * twice more to finish the round. To join the round, slip stitch into the third chain of the beginning chain-5.

Step 5: Third This counts as the first double crochet and corner space of two chains. Make 1 double crochet in the same stitch as the initial chain of five stitches.

In the following chain-2 corner space: Make 2 double crochet stitches, 2 chain stitches, and 2 double crochet stitches.

In the space of one chain between clusters, perform three double crochets.

For the remaining corners and sides, repeat the following pattern: In the next chain-2 space (corner space), perform 2 double crochet stitches, 2 chain stitches, and 2 double crochet stitches. In the chain-1 space between clusters, perform three double crochet stitches.After finishing all corners and sides, join the round with a slip stitch into the third chain of the initial chain-5.

Step 6: Beyond Round Four Continue the pattern from Round 3, adding additional rounds to increase the size of the doily and create space for adhering the Irish crochet rose motifs. You can enhance the design by adding more intricate stitching, picots, and other details.

Attaching the Rose Motifs is Step 7. Using a tapestry needle and thread of the same color as your rose, stitch the Irish crochet rose motifs onto the background of the doily. Position them in an aesthetically appealing arrangement and sew them in place securely.

Step 8: Completing Employ a tapestry needle to weave in any stray ends.

Blocking is the ninth (optional) step. To shape and flatten your doily, you can gently saturate it and attach it to a blocking mat, stretching and molding it into a circle. Permit it to cure thoroughly prior to removing the pegs.

And that concludes it! Your Irish Crochet Rose Doily is finished, exhibiting exquisite Irish crochet techniques and dazzling rose motifs. This sophisticated crochet project may require time and practice, but the end result will be a prized work of art. Best crochet wishes!

Guide to making Starburst Mandala Doily

Developing a Starburst. The mesmerizing starburst pattern of Mandala Doily is created with intricate stitching. Here is a step-by-step guide on how to create a beautiful Starburst Mandala Doily:

Material Required:

• Fine yarn or crochet thread • Crochet needle of 3.0 millimeters • Scissors

• Thread Needle

Initializing the Center To form a ring, create a magic ring or chain 4 and connect with a slip stitch.

Step 2: Round 1 Chain 1 (not counted as a stitch), then single crochet (sc) 12 times into the ring. You should have a total of 12 sutures.

Step 3: Round 2 Chain 3 (this counts as your first double crochet) and work 1 double crochet (dc) in the same stitch as your starting chain-3. In the following stitch, skip the next stitch and make 2 double crochets, 2 chains, and 2 double crochets to create a corner.

This pattern is repeated for the remaining stitches in the round: By skipping the next stitch, making 2 double crochets in the next stitch, skipping the next stitch, and making 2 double crochets, chain 2, and 2 double crochets in the next stitch, a corner is formed.

After finishing all corners and sides, join the round by working a slip stitch into the third chain of the initial chain-3.

Step 4: Round 3 Chain 3 (this counts as your first double crochet), then work 1 double crochet (dc) in the same stitch as your starting chain-3. In the corner space created by two chains, work two double crochets, two chains, and two double crochets.

In the space of one chain between clusters, work one double crochet.

For the remaining corners and sides, repeat the following pattern: In the next corner space formed by two chains, work two double crochets, two chains, and two double crochets. In the space of one chain between clusters, work one double crochet.

After finishing all corners and sides, join the round by working a slip stitch into the third chain of the initial chain-3.

Step 5: Beyond Round Four Continue the pattern from Round 3, adding additional rounds to expand the mandala starburst doily. Each round will contain more threads, chain spaces, and corners, resulting in a beautiful and intricate design.

Optional sixth stage: edging To complete the doily, you can add a border of your choosing. You may select a plain scalloped edge, picots, or any other decorative border that complements the design of the starburst mandala.

Step 7: Fasten Off Leave the yarn with a tail after cutting. Pull the tail through the final coil on the hook and tighten. Employ a tapestry needle to weave in any stray ends.

Optional eighth step: blocking To shape and flatten your doily, you can gently saturate it and attach it to a blocking mat, stretching and molding it into a circle. Permit it to cure thoroughly prior to removing the pegs.

And that concludes it! Your Starburst Mandala Doily is finished, with a captivating design that adds an artistic flourish to your home décor. Enjoy the process of creating this intricate crochet masterpiece by taking your time. Best crochet wishes!

Guide to making Tapestry Crochet Doily

The creation of a Tapestry Crochet Doily requires the use of multiple colors to create intricate patterns. Here is a step-by-step guide for crocheting a lovely Tapestry Crochet Doily:

Material Required:

- Fine yarn or crochet thread in at least two contrasting colors.

- 2.5 mm crochet implement

- Scissors

- Thread Needle

Step 1: Select a Design Choose or create a pattern for tapestry crochet for your doily. Tapestry crochet permits the creation of intricate, multicolored motifs. You can find patterns for crocheting tapestries in books and online resources, or you can create your own.

Step 2: Beginning the Centre To form a ring, create a magic ring or chain 4 and connect with a slip stitch.

Step 3: Round 1 Chain 1 (does not register as a stitch), then work single crochets (sc) into the ring until the first round of the pattern is complete. Utilize the dominant color for this round.

Step 4: Beyond Round Two In subsequent stages, you will utilize multiple colors. Join the new color to the thread at the beginning of the round. As you work, you will incorporate the unused color into the patterns. Follow the specified color variations in the pattern and crochet the necessary stitches accordingly.

To incorporate an unused color into the stitches: When switching colors, place the current color behind your work and grab the new color. As you make loops, crochet over the unemployed color. This method conceals the unused color, resulting in an organized design.

5. Completion of the Pattern Continue crocheting each round in accordance with the selected tapestry crochet pattern. Pay close attention to color changes and stitch counts to ensure that your design is accurate.

Optional sixth stage: edging To complete the doily, you can add a simple border or decorative outlining in the dominant color or a contrasting color. This will give the doily a refined appearance and frame the intricate crochet tapestry design.

Step 7: Fasten Off Leave the yarn with a tail after cutting. Pull the tail through the final coil on the hook and tighten. Employ a tapestry needle to weave in any stray ends.

Optional eighth step: blocking To shape and flatten your doily, you can gently saturate it and attach it to a blocking mat, stretching and molding it into a circle. Permit it to cure thoroughly prior to removing the pegs.

In conclusion, there you have it! Your Tapestry Crochet Doily is finished, showcasing an impressive design accomplished through the skillful use of color transitions. The craft of tapestry crochet enables the creation of breathtaking, one-of-a-kind patterns that are certain to be admired. Take pleasure in the process of creating this exquisite crochet tapestry. Best crochet wishes!

Guide to making Victorian Ruffled Doily

The creation of a Victorian Ruffled Doily requires intricate designs and delicate stitching. Here is a step-by-step guide on how to create a beautiful Victorian Ruffled Doily:

Material Required:

• Fine yarn or thread for crocheting • 2.0 mm crochet needle

• Scissors

• Thread Needle

Initializing the Center To form a ring, create a magic ring or chain 4 and connect with a slip stitch.

Step 2: First Round Chain 1 (does not register as a stitch), then work single crochets (sc) into the ring until the first round is complete. You should have a total of 12 sutures.

Step 3: Round 2 Chain 3 (this counts as your first double crochet) and work 2 double crochets (dc) in the same stitch as your starting chain-3. Skipping the next stitch, make 3 double crochets in the next stitch, followed by 2 chains and 3 double crochets to create a corner.

This pattern is repeated for the remaining stitches in the round: By skipping the next stitch, making 3 double crochets in the next stitch, skipping the next stitch, and making 3 double crochets, chain 2, and 3 double crochets in the next stitch, a corner is formed.

After completing all corners and sides, join the round with a slip stitch into the top of the commencing chain-3.

Step 4: Round 3 Chain 3 (this counts as your first double crochet) and work 1 double crochet in each of the next 2 threads. In the corner space created by two chains, work three double crochets, two chains, and three double crochets.

In the next chain-1 intercluster space: Perform a double crochet stitch in each of the next three threads.

For the remaining corners and sides, repeat the following pattern: In the next corner space created by two chains, work three double crochets, two chains, and three double crochets. In the next chain-1 space between clusters, double crochet each of the following three threads.

After completing all corners and sides, join the round with a slip stitch into the top of the commencing chain-3.

Fifth Step: Ruffled Edging For the scalloped edge, we will work exclusively in the back loops. In the same stitch, chain 1 (this does not count as a stitch) and work 1 single crochet (sc).

In the back loop only of every stitch around, work 1 single crochet, and in each corner space created by 2 chains, work 1 single crochet, 3 chains, and 1 single crochet.

To finalize the ruffled edge, slip stitch into the initial single crochet.

Step 6: Fasten Off Leave the yarn with a tail after cutting. Pull the tail through the final coil on the hook and tighten. Employ a tapestry needle to weave in any stray ends.

Optional seventh step: blocking. To shape and flatten your doily, you can gently saturate it and attach it to a blocking mat, stretching and molding it into a circle. Permit it to cure thoroughly prior to removing the pegs.

In conclusion, there you have it! Your Victorian Ruffled Doily is finished, displaying a lovely design with delicate ruffles that add a refined addition to your home décor. Enjoy the process of crocheting this intricate work of art. Best crochet wishes!

Guide to making Celtic Knot Doily

The creation of a Celtic Knot Doily requires intricate stitching and a pattern that resembles the interwoven patterns of Celtic knots. Here is a step-by-step guide on how to create a beautiful Celtic Knot Doily:

Material Required:

- Fine yarn or crochet thread • Crochet needle of 2.5 millimeters • Scissors

- Thread Needle

Initializing the Center To form a ring, create a magic ring or chain 4 and connect with a slip stitch.

Step 2: Round 1 Chain 3 (counts as the first double crochet) and work 11 double crochets (dc) into the ring. You should have a total of 12 threads, including the initial chain-3.

Step 3: Round 2 Chain 3 (this counts as your first double crochet) and work 1 double crochet (dc) in the same stitch as your starting chain-3. Perform two double crochet stitches in each of the next eleven stitches around the ring. To join the round, slip stitch into the top of the commencing chain-3. You should have a total of 24 sutures.

Step 4: Round 3 Chain 3 (this counts as your first double crochet), then work 1 double crochet (dc) in the same stitch as your starting chain-3. Perform two double crochet stitches in the next stitch. In the following stitch, perform 1 double crochet, 2 chain stitches, and 1 double crochet to create a corner.

This pattern is repeated for the remaining stitches in the round: Create a corner by working 2 double crochets in the next stitch, followed by 1 double crochet, 2 chains, and 1 double crochet in the next stitch.

After completing all corners and sides, join the round with a slip stitch into the top of the commencing chain-3.

Fifth Step: Celtic Knot Pattern Using specialized stitching techniques, the Celtic Knot will be created in successive cycles. Follow the pattern's specific instructions to create the interwoven knot motif. Typically, this is accomplished by combining double crochets, chains, and slip threads to produce the desired knot pattern.

Step 6: Beyond Round Four Continue the pattern for the Celtic Knot design in each round, incorporating increasingly intricate details and stitches to form interwoven patterns.

Optional Step 7: Edges To complete the doily, you can add a simple border or decorative outlining in the dominant color or a contrasting color. This will lend a refined appearance to the doily and frame the intricate Celtic Knot design.

Step 8: Fasten Off Leave the yarn with a tail after cutting. Pull the tail through the final coil on the hook and tighten. Employ a tapestry needle to weave in any stray ends.

Blocking is the ninth (optional) step. To shape and flatten your doily, you can gently saturate it and attach it to a blocking mat, stretching and molding it into a circle. Permit it to cure thoroughly prior to removing the pegs.

And that concludes it! Your Celtic Knot Doily is finished, displaying an intricate pattern that resembles the beauty of Celtic knots. This doily may require patience and skill to create, but the end result will be a beautiful crochet masterpiece. Take pleasure in creating this exquisite Celtic Knot Doily. Best crochet wishes!

Guide to making Pineapple Lace Doily

The creation of a Pineapple Lace Doily requires working with pineapple motifs to create an intricate, delicate design. Here is a step-by-step guide on how to make a beautiful Pineapple Lace Doily:

Material Required:

- Fine yarn or crochet thread • Crochet needle of 2.0 millimeters • Scissors

- Thread Needle

Initializing the Center To form a ring, create a magic ring or chain six stitches and connect with a slip stitch.

Phase 2: Round 1 Chain 3 (this counts as your first double crochet), then work 11 double crochets (dc) into the ring (this counts as your first double crochet). You should have a total of 12 threads, including the initial chain-3.

Step 3: Round 2 In the same stitch as the initial chain-1, perform one single crochet (sc). Chain 5, omit the next stitch, and single crochet in the stitch that follows.

This pattern is repeated for the remaining stitches in the round: Chain 5, omit the next stitch, and single crochet in the stitch that follows.

To join the round, slip stitch into the first single crochet.

Step 4: Third Slip stitch into the first space created by five chains. Chain 3 (this counts as your first double crochet), then work 2 double crochet stitches in the same chain-5 space. Chain 5, then work three double crochet stitches in the next chain-5 space.

Repeat the pattern below for the remaining chain-5 spaces in the round. Chain 5, then work three double crochet stitches in the next chain-5 space.

To join the round, slip stitch into the top of the commencing chain-3.

Step 5: Beyond Round Four Continue the pineapple motif pattern according to each round's specific design instructions. Each subsequent round will typically increase the number of chain-5 spaces and double crochets in each space, resulting in increasingly intricate pineapple lace motifs.

Optional sixth stage: edging You can complete the doily with a simple scalloped edge or any other decorative edge of your choosing. This will lend a refined appearance to the doily and enhance its intricate design.

Step 7: Fasten Off Leave the yarn with a tail after cutting. Pull the tail through the final coil on the hook and tighten.

Employ a tapestry needle to weave in any stray ends.

Optional eighth step: blocking To shape and flatten your doily, you can gently saturate it and attach it to a blocking mat, stretching and molding it into a circle. Permit it to cure thoroughly prior to removing the pegs.

And that concludes it! Your finished Pineapple Lace Doily features intricate pineapple motifs that add elegance to any surface. Creating this doily may require patience and attention to detail, but the end result will be a breathtaking crochet work of art. Appreciate the process of creating this lovely Pineapple Lace Doily. Best crochet wishes!

CHAPTER SIX

Incorporating Beads and Embellishments into your doilies

Beads and embellishments can lend a touch of elegance, glitter, and texture to your crochet creations by being incorporated into your dolls. Here is a guide for doing so:

Material Required:

• Fine yarn or crochet thread • Crochet needle measuring 2.5 mm

• Beads or adornments of your choosing

• Beading needle (for tiny beads) • Sewing needle and thread (for larger embellishments).

Selecting Beads and Embellishments in Step 1. Choose beads or embellishments that complement the design and colors of your dolls. Small seed beads can be used to create delicate accents, while larger beads, sequins, and other embellishments can be used to create bolder statements.

Step 2: Add Beads During Crochet You can add gemstones to crochet using one of two methods:

Method 1: Stringing Beads in Advance Before beginning your creation, string the beads onto the twine or thread beforehand. When you reach the seam where you want to add a bead, slide a bead onto the hook and complete the stitch to secure it. This technique is most effective with tiny beads.

Technique Two: Crochet with Beads Insert the hook through the bead or attachment loop and draw the yarn through the thread for larger beads or embellishments. Perform the suture as normal. This procedure permits the direct attachment of larger embellishments to the fabric while crocheting.

Third Step: Crocheting Specific Bead Patterns Beads can be incorporated into particular patterns or motifs to create spectacular effects. For instance, you can add beads to the center of a floral motif, along the edge of a doily, or in a particular order to create a unique pattern.

Step 4: Attaching Accessories Following Crochet If you would rather not crochet with beads, you can add them later. To sew on larger embellishments, use a needle and thread that complements the color of your project. Sew the beads or embellishments to the crochet fabric for a secure attachment.

Experiment and investigate Experiment with various jewels, sequins, and embellishments without fear. Mix and match colors and sizes to create personalized designs that are unique. You can design symmetrical patterns, random sequences, or your own unique style.

Optional sixth step: blocking If the embellishments on your dolls are delicate, consider blocking them meticulously. Dampen the item, reform it into the desired shape, and attach it to a blocking mat. Permit it to cure thoroughly prior to removing the pegs.

Be creative and remember to have fun when incorporating beads and embellishments into your dolls. They provide limitless customization options and can convert your crochet creations into exquisite works of art. Best crochet wishes!

Tips for Finishing and Blocking Doilies

Finishing and blocking are necessary stages for giving your crochet creations a polished and professional appearance. Here are some useful finishing and blocking suggestions for your dolls:

Finishing:

1. Weave in Ends Neatly: After completing your doll, use a tapestry needle to weave in all loose ends. To

prevent unraveling, secure the yarn by weaving it through several threads in different directions.

Consider barring individual motifs as you go when working on intricate doilies or crafts with multiple motifs. This will simplify the final blocking procedure and produce a more uniform outcome.

Trimming Excess Yarn: After weaving in the ends, trim any excess yarn close to the threads to maintain a neat and orderly appearance for your doll.

4.Adding Embellishments: If you intend to add beads, sequins, or other embellishments, secure them to the doll using a stitching needle and thread that matches. Ensure that they are securely affixed to prevent them from detaching during use or laundering.

5. Blocking damp vs. Dry: Based on the yarn or thread used and your personal preference, decide whether to block your doll damp or dry. Wet blocking entails wetting the marionette prior to securing it in position for shaping, whereas dry blocking does not involve any moisture.

Blocking:

Understanding Fiber Content Various fibers and strands respond to blocking differently. Natural fibers, such as cotton or wool, are more elastic and respond well to blocking, whereas man-made fibers may require more attention.

Soaking the Doily: Soak the doily in cool water for 15 to 20 minutes for damp blocking. Carefully drain out excess water without wringing or twisting the delicate fabric.

Use T-pins or blocking pins that are resistant to corrosion to secure the trolley to a blocking mat or polystyrene board. Stretch and form the marionette to the desired dimensions, paying close attention to maintaining straight edges and symmetry.

Use obstructing mats or cloths under the trolley to prevent moisture from penetrating and to safeguard your work surface.

Allow Sufficient Drying Time: Allow the marionette to dry completely before removing the pins. This can take anywhere from a few hours to an entire day, depending on the yarn, humidity, and fabric thickness.

6. Steam Blocking (For Acrylic Yarn): Use steam blocking for acrylic yarn or strands that do not respond well to damp blocking. To delicately shape and establish the threads without contacting the doll, hover a steam iron over it without touching it.

7. Handle Delicate Motifs With Care For dolls with delicate motifs or intricate edges, use blocking wires or insert them through the edges prior to fastening in order to maintain the desired shape.

Remember that blocking is a fantastic way to improve the appearance of your crochet dolls by ensuring that they lie evenly, retain their shape, and showcase the intricate patterns you've created. Finishing and blocking your crochet creations properly will add that final element of elegance. Best crochet wishes!

Enhancing the Beauty of Your Finished Doilies

Consider incorporating the following suggestions and techniques to enhance the attractiveness of your completed dolls and make them stand out as true crochet masterpieces:

As mentioned previously, blocking is a crucial phase in completing your dolls. It evens out the threads, molds the project, and gives it a refined, professional appearance.

After blocking, flatten your doilies gingerly with a steam iron on the lowest setting. This will further level out any remaining creases and give your work a clean finish.

Add strategically placed jewels, sequins, or other embellishments to your dolls to accentuate specific features. Beads can add a touch of sophistication and shimmer, while sequins can produce a scintillating effect.

Consider adding decorative edgings, such as picots, shells, or lace, to your dolls. The addition of edgings to a project can give it a finished appearance and a hint of sophistication.

5. Color Combinations: Choose colors with care. Experiment with various color combinations to produce distinctive and aesthetically pleasing results. A carefully selected color scheme can enhance the overall attractiveness of your dolls.

Size of Thread: Experiment with various thread diameters to accomplish various effects. The use of thicker threads can result in bolder and more substantial designs, whereas the use of finer threads produces intricate and fragile projects.

7. Try Different Patterns: Try out novel and challenging patterns without fear. There are numerous crochet patterns available, ranging from classic to contemporary designs. Learn new

techniques and make dolls that are diverse and eye-catching.

Texture: Experiment with texture by combining crochet stitches. Adding texture to your dolls can add dimension and appeal.

Pay close attention to the finishing touches, such as weaving in ends and trimming excess yarn. These concluding details can make a substantial difference in your project's final appearance.

Display your completed dolls in an attractive manner. Consider framing them, arranging them in a decorative vase, or using them as table centerpieces. Displaying your crochet works can highlight their attractiveness and add a touch of sophistication to your residence.

Invest time in taking high-quality photographs if you intend to display your dolls online or in a portfolio. With proper illumination and attention to detail, your work can appear even more impressive.

Remember that the pleasure of crochet rests not only in the act of creating, but also in displaying your completed works. Take pride in your work and acknowledge the exquisiteness of your dolls. In every item you create, your creativity and hard work will be evident. Best crochet wishes!

Made in the USA
Columbia, SC
05 July 2025